Entrepreneurs Guide to
Business Plan

Understanding business before you take the leap

SresQUEST

Table of Content

This guide is dedicated to all the entrepreneurs out there who are taking the leap of faith and turning their dreams into reality. Starting a business is not easy, but with the right mindset and a solid plan in place, anything is possible. This book is a tool to help you navigate the challenges and opportunities that come with entrepreneurship, and to help you build a business that will stand the test of time. May this guide serve as a valuable resource as you embark on your own entrepreneurial journey.

I would like to pay tribute to my late father, P.P. Sridharan, who taught me the importance of hard work, determination, and perseverance. His unwavering support and guidance were essential in shaping my life's journey. I am forever grateful for the wisdom and encouragement he provided, and I feel his blessings with me at all times. He instilled in me a belief that has grown stronger over time, becoming my guiding principle: **"One who seeks, finds the way."** This belief has helped me to persevere through setbacks, and continue to strive towards my goals.

A good business plan **doesn't guarantee success** of your business **but it certainly increases** the chances of success

Prologue

Starting a business is an exciting and challenging journey. It takes determination, hard work, and a solid plan to turn an idea into a successful venture. This book, "Entrepreneur's Guide to Business Plan," is designed to be a comprehensive guide for aspiring entrepreneurs who are looking to turn their vision into a reality.

In this book, you will learn the essential steps to creating a business plan that will help you secure funding, attract investors, and guide your business to success. We will cover topics such as understanding fundamentals of business and business plan.

I have learned firsthand the importance of a well-crafted business plan. I have also made mistakes along the way and understood the need of business plan to help avoid the common pitfall on your journey.

This book is not just a guide, it is a companion that will help you navigate the complex and ever-changing landscape of entrepreneurship. It is my hope that it will inspire you to take the first step towards realizing your dream and becoming a successful entrepreneur.

As the business world evolves and new technologies and trends emerge, it can be difficult to keep up with the latest developments. But while the specifics of how we conduct business may change over time, **the fundamentals of what it takes to create a successful venture remain the same.** This is where "Entrepreneur's Guide to Business Plan" comes in.

So, let's begin this journey together, let's create a business plan that will turn your idea into reality.

A JOURNEY OF A
THOUSAND MILES
MUST BEGIN WITH A
SINGLE STEP.

LAO TZU

Google is the perfect source for quick learning, search on any topic of your interest and in seconds you have hundreds and thousands of pages to browse through. but google also possess a challenge in searching out the right knowledge you seek. And many at times you end up spending more time not knowing what exactly you need.

That's why with my little experience that led me from working for a company to becoming an entrepreneur, I gathered experiences on the way for last 30yrs meeting challenges and repeatedly falling and standing again,

During the course of my journey, it was much latter I understood the importance of writing a BUSINESS PLAN "before stepping into the vast space of entrepreneurship, All entrepreneurs of the world tend to be crazy, trying to accomplish things which most around them wouldn't dare to even dream.

Entrepreneurs journey starts with a dream to solve a common problem, or to enhance everyday experience in a human life,

To make this dream a successful reality an entrepreneur needs to break this dream idea into smaller targets and elaborate these targets to form a road map that helps to constructively achieve and turn the dream into a reality.

BUSINESS PLAN is the process to transfer **"what's in mind"** onto a written expression, a step-by-step guide to build your dream into successful organization.

I have managed to cover most important and fundamental topics that would help a person planning to jump into the world of entrepreneurship, life is a wonderful teacher so one needs to be open to new learnings as you progress, it's all about moving on. creating experiences for yourself as well as for others.

"IDEAS ARE DIME A DOZEN"
PEOPLE WHO IMPLEMENT THEM
ARE PRICELESS

MARY KAY ASH

It's true that having a good idea is an important first step, but it's often the implementation of that idea that determines its success or failure. Many entrepreneurs and business leaders have emphasized the importance of taking action and following through on ideas in order to achieve success. **It's not enough to simply have a good idea**; you have to be able to put that idea into action and make it a reality. This often requires a combination of hard work, perseverance, and the ability to adapt and pivot when things don't go as planned. Ultimately, it's the combination of a good idea and the ability to successfully implement it that can lead to success.

IF YOU SET YOUR GOALS RIDICULOUSLY HIGH, AND IT'S A FAILURE, YOU WILL FAIL ABOVE EVERYONE ELSE'S SUCCESS.

JAMES CAMERON

Here are 1st few basic steps to start a business anywhere in the world, registrations, statutory compliance, laws will vary as per the country you intent to start your business, always don't hesitate to take a professional help.

- ➤ Consult with an auditor and legal advisor to determine the best business structure and navigate legal requirements. (E.g.: partnership, private limited, LLP, etc.)

- ➤ Secure a location through a rental or lease agreement.

- ➤ Register your company name and logo under "TRADE MARK".

- ➤ Obtain any necessary licenses or permits specific to your business.

- ➤ Comply with health and safety and employment laws.

- ➤ Register for taxes and set up a business bank account.

- ➤ Create a business plan and financial projections.

- ➤ Seek professional advice as needed.

Most entrepreneurs start a business based on their gut feeling intuition or their experience.

Starting a business based on an entrepreneur's experience, confidence, and intuition can be a valid approach, but it is important to have a solid business plan in place to ensure sustainable growth and scalability. A business plan can help an entrepreneur to identify and evaluate opportunities, set goals, and develop strategies to achieve them. It is especially important once the business reaches stability and the entrepreneur wants to replicate its success and transform it into a well-organized company.

A business or organization should be able to run smoothly even if the owner / founder is not available, and this is made possible by having a well-designed business plan in place. A business plan should outline the various functions of the business, the roles and responsibilities of each team member, and the procedures for running the business on a day-to-day basis. It should also include a clear succession plan and contingencies for unexpected events. In this way, the business can continue to operate even if the owner / founder is absent, and it will be more likely to maintain its stability and growth even in his absence.

Important trait for entrepreneurs

Decision making and owning the outcome of those decisions is an **important trait for entrepreneurs**. As an entrepreneur, you are responsible for making a wide range of decisions that can have a significant impact on your business. This can include everything from deciding what products or services to offer, how to price them, how to market and sell them, and how to manage and grow your business. Being able to make informed and confident decisions, and then being willing to take responsibility for the outcome of those decisions, is crucial for the success of any entrepreneur. It requires the ability to gather and analyze information, weigh the pros and cons of different options, and then make a decision that you believe is best for your business. It also requires the courage to take action and the resilience to learn from any mistakes or setbacks that may occur as a result of your decisions.

As a leader, it is important to take responsibility for the failures that occur within the organization and to use them as opportunities for learning and improvement. At the same time, it is also important to celebrate and acknowledge the successes of the team, and to attribute them to the hard work and contributions of the team members. This type of leadership style is known as "servant leadership" which emphasizes putting the needs of the team members first and creating an environment in which they can thrive. By being humble and supportive, a leader can build trust and respect among the team members, which can lead to better performance and more successful outcomes.

Ability to multitask

Another vital trait for a person aspiring to do business is they must have the ability to learn and multitask in order to be successful. They need to be able to quickly adapt to new information and changing circumstances, and they must be able to juggle multiple tasks and projects at once. Building these abilities can be accomplished through practice and experience, as well as by seeking out opportunities to learn new skills and take on new challenges. Additionally, some key strategies to help improve multitasking abilities include setting clear priorities, breaking tasks down into manageable chunks, and using tools and technology to automate or streamline certain tasks.

Find a balance between your passion and market need

It is important for an entrepreneur to find a balance between their passion and what the market needs when starting a business. This balance is important because it can help to ensure that the business is both personally rewarding for the entrepreneur and viable in the market.

Passion is important because it can fuel the entrepreneur's motivation and drive to succeed. When an entrepreneur is passionate about their business, they are more likely to put in the time and effort required to make it a success. However, it is also important for the business to address a need or solve a problem in the market in order to be viable. Without a market need, it may be difficult for the business to attract and retain customers, which is essential for its success.

Finding the right balance between passion and market need can be challenging, but it is an important consideration for any entrepreneur. By identifying and addressing a market need while pursuing a passion, entrepreneurs can create businesses that are both personally rewarding and successful.

Understanding market fit of your business idea:

Understanding the market fit of a product is an important step in starting a business. It helps you determine if there is a demand for your product and if it will be successful in the market. There are a few key factors to consider when evaluating the market fit of a product:

Target market: Identify the specific group of people who will be interested in your product. This includes factors such as demographics, location, and needs.

Competition: Research other products or services that are similar to yours, and consider how your product compares in terms of price, quality, and unique features.

Demand: Determine if there is a need for your product in the market. This can involve surveying potential customers or analyzing data on similar products.

Marketing strategy: Develop a plan for promoting your product and reaching your target market. Consider the channels you will use, such as social media, advertising, or partnerships.

By thoroughly evaluating these factors, you can get a better understanding of the market fit for your product and make informed decisions about your business.

According to a report published by Dell Technologies and authored by the **Institute for The Future** (IFTF) and a panel of 20 tech, business and academic experts from around the world, states that 85 per cent of the jobs that will exist in 2030 haven't even been invented yet.

Always be proactive to learn:

It is true that new technologies and innovations can lead to the creation of new industries and job markets. As an entrepreneur, it is important to stay informed about new developments in your industry and be open to learning and adapting to new technologies and ideas. This can help you to stay competitive and find new opportunities for growth.

It is also important to be proactive in seeking out new knowledge and skills that may be relevant to your business. This may involve taking courses or attending workshops, networking with other professionals, or simply keeping up with industry news and developments. By constantly learning and staying up-to-date, you can position yourself and your business for success in an ever-changing environment.

Don't worry about failure, you only have to be right once.

DREW HOUSTONT

Dare to dream big:

It can be beneficial for entrepreneurs to **aspire and dream big**, as having a clear vision and ambitious goals can help to provide motivation and direction. Setting big goals can help entrepreneurs to stay focused and committed to their business, and to stay motivated even in the face of challenges or setbacks.

Having a big dream can also help entrepreneurs to stay engaged and energized, and to see the bigger picture of what they are working towards. This can help to keep them motivated and inspired, even when the day-to-day work of running a business becomes challenging or tedious.

However, it is also important for entrepreneurs to be realistic and to be aware of the resources and limitations that they have. While it is important to aim high, it is also important to be strategic and to plan carefully in order to achieve success. This may involve setting smaller, intermediate goals that can help to build momentum and progress towards the bigger dream over time.

Starting a Business:

Starting a business becoming an entrepreneur can be a challenging and risky endeavor, and it's not for everyone. It requires a lot of hard work, dedication, and a willingness to take on risks and uncertainties. Many people prefer the stability and security of working for others, and that's perfectly fine.

That being said, starting a business can also be extremely rewarding. It allows you to be your own boss, pursue your passions, and create something of your own. If you have a good idea and the drive and determination to see it through, starting a business can be a fulfilling and rewarding experience.

Ultimately, the decision to start a business or work for someone else is a personal one that depends on your individual goals, skills, and **risk tolerance**. It's important to carefully consider your options and make a decision that's right for you.

> ## Risk more than others think is safe. Dream more than others think is practical.

HOWARD SCHULTZ

Benefits of doing business:

Doing business can provide many benefits for individuals and society as a whole. Some of the potential benefits of doing business include:

Personal fulfillment: Starting and running a business can be a rewarding and challenging experience that allows you to use your skills, creativity, and problem-solving abilities.

Financial rewards: Successful businesses can generate profits and provide financial security for the owner and their employees.

Job creation: Businesses can create jobs and provide employment opportunities for people in the community.

Economic development: Businesses can contribute to the overall economic development of a community or region by providing goods and services, generating tax revenue, and attracting additional investment.

Innovation: Businesses can drive innovation and progress by introducing new products and services, improving existing ones, and finding creative solutions to problems.

Social impact: Businesses can also have a positive social impact by addressing social and environmental issues, such as providing products or services that benefit underserved communities or promoting sustainability.

Overall, doing business can provide personal and financial benefits for individuals and contribute to the overall economic and social development of a community or society.

I DON'T LOOK TO JUMP OVER 7- FOOT BARS. I LOOK FOR 1-FOOT BARS THAT I CAN STEP OVER.

WARREN BUFFETT

Importance of Understanding fundamentals of business:

Understanding the fundamentals of business is important for an entrepreneur to write a business plan because it helps to ensure that the plan is grounded in sound business principles and practices. A business plan is a detailed roadmap for starting and operating a business, and it should outline the key elements of the business, such as its target market, products or services, financial projections, and marketing and sales strategies. To create a successful and realistic business plan, an entrepreneur needs to have a deep understanding of the fundamental principles of business, such as marketing, finance, operations, and management. This knowledge will help the entrepreneur to make informed decisions about the direction and goals of the business and to develop strategies that are likely to be effective in achieving those goals. Additionally, having a strong understanding of business fundamentals can help an entrepreneur to identify and assess potential risks and opportunities, and to adapt to changes in the market or business environment.

Delegation and accountability:

Delegation of work and accountability are important for entrepreneurs for a number of reasons.

First, delegation allows entrepreneurs to focus on their strengths and delegate tasks that they are not as skilled at or that take up too much of their time. This can help them be more productive and efficient, allowing them to better manage their workload and grow their business.

Second, delegation can help build a strong team and create a sense of ownership and accountability among team members. When team members are given specific tasks and responsibilities, they are more likely to feel invested in the success of the business and motivated to perform at their best.

Finally, accountability is important for entrepreneurs because it helps to ensure that tasks are completed on time and to the required standard. This can help the business operate smoothly and avoid any delays or setbacks.

Overall, delegation of work and accountability are crucial for entrepreneurs because they allow them to focus on their strengths, build a strong team, and ensure that tasks are completed effectively and efficiently.

Importance of "Discipline"

Discipline is important when starting a business for a number of reasons.

Time management: As a business owner, you will have a lot on your plate and it's important to prioritize your tasks and manage your time effectively. Discipline helps you stay focused on the tasks at hand and ensures that you are using your time efficiently.

Goal-setting: Discipline helps you set clear goals for your business and stay focused on achieving them. By setting clear goals and working towards them consistently, you can help ensure the success of your business.

Decision-making: Discipline can also help you make better decisions for your business. By considering the long-term consequences of your actions and making decisions based on a well-thought-out plan, you can help your business stay on track and avoid unnecessary risks.

Personal development: Being discipline can also help you grow as a person and improve your personal and professional skills. By setting goals for yourself and working towards them, you can become more organized, focused, and motivated, which can help you achieve success in all areas of your life.

Discipline is a key factor in the success of any business, as it helps you manage your time, set and achieve goals, make better decisions, and continuously improve your skills and abilities.

Disciplinary factors:

There are several important disciplinary factors and key points that aspiring entrepreneurs should consider:

Passion: As an entrepreneur, you need to be passionate about your business idea. This will help you stay motivated and committed to your goals, even when faced with challenges.

Persistence: Being an entrepreneur requires a high level of persistence. You may encounter setbacks and obstacles along the way, and it's important to be able to persevere and keep moving forward.

Flexibility: The business world is constantly changing, and as an entrepreneur, you need to be able to adapt and adjust to new circumstances.

Creativity: Entrepreneurs often need to come up with innovative solutions to problems, so being creative is an important skill to have.

Risk-taking: Starting a business requires taking risks, and as an entrepreneur, you need to be comfortable with the idea of taking calculated risks in order to succeed.

Time management: As an entrepreneur, you will likely have a lot of responsibilities and tasks to manage. It's important to be able to prioritize and use your time efficiently.

Resourcefulness: Entrepreneurs need to be resourceful and able to make the most of the resources available to them.

Leadership: As an entrepreneur, you will likely be responsible for leading and managing a team. It's important to be a strong leader and have or develop good communication skills.

Networking: Building a strong network of contacts and relationships can be can be beneficial for an entrepreneur. It's important to be proactive in building and maintaining these connections.

Financial management: As an entrepreneur, you will need to manage your financial resources carefully. This includes budgeting, forecasting, and making smart financial decisions.

Ethics in business:

Ethics in business refers to the principles and values that guide the behavior of individuals and organizations in the business world. A good business person is someone who operates with a strong sense of ethics, which includes honesty, fairness, and integrity.

Some specific characteristics of a good business person with strong ethics might include:

Honesty: A good business person is honest and transparent in their dealings with others, including customers, employees, partners, and competitors.

Fairness: A good business person treats all stakeholders fairly and equally, and avoids discriminating against anyone on the basis of factors such as race, gender, religion, or nationality.

Responsibility: A good business person takes responsibility for their actions and their impact on others, and works to minimize any negative consequences of their business practices.

Respect: A good business person treats others with respect, regardless of their position or status, and promotes a culture of mutual respect within their organization.

Sustainability: A good business person recognizes the long-term impact of their actions on the environment and society, and works to minimize any negative consequences of their business practices.

A good business person is someone who upholds high ethical standards and values in all aspects of their work, and strives to contribute positively to the world around them.

Focus in what you want to achieve:

Focus is an important trait for any entrepreneur to have in their journey. It allows you to concentrate your energy and resources on specific tasks or goals, which can help you to achieve success more quickly and efficiently.

Here are a few reasons why focus is so important in the entrepreneurial journey:

It helps you to avoid distractions: Entrepreneurs are often faced with a wide range of competing demands and distractions, such as emails, phone calls, and meetings. By focusing on one task at a time, you can avoid getting sidetracked and stay on track with your goals.

It allows you to make better decisions: When you are focused, you are better able to assess situations and make informed decisions. This can help you to identify opportunities, avoid pitfalls, and make progress towards your goals.

It increases productivity: When you focus on one task at a time, you are able to work more efficiently and get more done in less time.

This can help you to achieve your goals more quickly and free up time to work on other important tasks.

It helps you to maintain momentum: Keeping your focus on your goals allows you to maintain momentum and stay motivated. This can be particularly important when you encounter setbacks or challenges, as it helps you to stay focused on the end result and continue moving forward.

In summary, focus is a crucial trait for entrepreneurs to have in their journey. By maintaining focus, you can avoid distractions, make better decisions, increase productivity, and maintain momentum towards achieving your goals.

GOOD BUSINESS
LEADERS CREATE A
VISION, ARTICULATE
THE VISION,
PASSIONATELY OWN
THE VISION, AND
RELENTLESSLY DRIVE
IT TO COMPLETION.

JACK WELCH

Importance of an entrepreneur's "vision and mission"

An entrepreneur's vision and mission should be based on their values and long-term goals for their business. The vision is the long-term, aspirational goal that the entrepreneur wants to achieve, while the mission is the purpose or reason for the business's existence.

The vision and mission should be closely tied to the unique value proposition of the business and the needs and wants of the target market. They should also align with the strengths and capabilities of the business, as well as the entrepreneur's personal values and motivations.

An entrepreneur's vision and mission should be based on their values, goals, and the needs and interests of their target audience. The vision should be a long-term, aspirational statement that describes the impact the entrepreneur wants to have on the world or the industry in which they are operating. The mission, on the other hand, is a statement that outlines the specific actions the entrepreneur will take to achieve their vision.

Here are some tips for framing an entrepreneur's vision and mission:

Start by identifying your values and goals. What are the guiding principles that drive you and your business? What do you hope to achieve through your work?

Consider the needs and interests of your target audience. What problems are they facing, and how can your business help solve them?

Keep your vision and mission concise and clear. Avoid using jargon or industry-specific language that may not be understood by a broad audience.

Make sure your vision and mission are aligned with your business goals and strategy. Your vision should be a long-term statement, but your mission should focus on the specific actions you will take to achieve it.

Review and revise your vision and mission regularly to ensure they remain relevant and aligned with the changing needs of your business and your target audience.

Observing and Learning from NATURE

There are a few reasons why everything in life and in nature seems to be governed by rules and discipline.

One reason is that rules and discipline help to establish order and predictability. When things follow a set of rules, it becomes easier for people (or other living things) to understand how the world works and to predict what will happen in different situations. This can make it easier to plan and make decisions, and it can also help to prevent chaos and confusion.

Another reason is that rules and discipline often help to ensure the well-being and survival of individuals and communities. For example, rules that govern behavior in social groups help to prevent conflict and promote cooperation, which can be essential for the group's survival. In nature, the laws of physics and the behaviors of different species help to maintain balance and stability in ecosystems, which is necessary for the survival of all the organisms that live there.

Finally, rules and discipline can also be used to encourage growth and development. For example, in a human society, rules and laws can be used to establish standards for education, work, and personal behavior that can help people to reach their full potential. Similarly, in nature, the inherent rules and patterns of growth and development help plants and animals to grow and thrive.

In many ways, running a business can be compared to operating within a set of rules and following a discipline in order to achieve a desired outcome. This is because a business is an organization that is created to provide goods or services to customers and to make a profit. In order to do this effectively and sustainably, it is important for a business to have a clear set of goals and objectives, and to develop strategies and processes for achieving those goals.

This often requires following certain rules and disciplines, such as adhering to regulations, managing financial resources carefully, and maintaining good relationships with customers, employees, and other stakeholders.

There are many factors that can influence the success or failure of a business, and having a set of rules and disciplines in place can help to provide a sense of stability and direction. This can be especially important in times of uncertainty or change, when a clear set of guidelines can help to guide decision-making and keep the business on track. At the same time, it is also important for businesses to be adaptable and open to change, as the business environment is constantly evolving and it may be necessary to adjust strategies and processes in order to stay competitive.

MOST PEOPLE OVERESTIMATE WHAT THEY CAN DO IN ONE YEAR AND UNDERESTIMATE WHAT THEY CAN DO IN TEN YEARS.

BILL GATES

Entrepreneurs attitude and mindset:

Having a "will not die" attitude can be an important mindset for entrepreneurs to have, as it can help them stay focused and motivated during difficult times. This attitude involves a determination to keep going and find creative solutions to overcome challenges, even when things seem insurmountable.

Here are a few ways in which a "will not die" attitude can be beneficial for entrepreneurs:

Overcoming setbacks and challenges: Entrepreneurs often face a variety of challenges and setbacks, such as financial difficulties, regulatory hurdles, and competitive pressures. Having a "will not die" attitude can help entrepreneurs stay motivated and focused on finding solutions to these challenges, rather than giving up.

Building resilience: Entrepreneurship can be a rollercoaster ride, and it's important to have the resilience to handle the ups and downs. A "will not die" attitude can help entrepreneurs develop this resilience and bounce back from failures or setbacks more quickly.

Maintaining motivation: Being an entrepreneur can be demanding and it's important to stay motivated and focused on the long-term vision. A "will not die" attitude can help entrepreneurs stay motivated and keep working towards their goals, even when faced with setbacks and challenges.

Staying focused: Starting a business often involves taking on many different projects and tasks, some of which may be complex and time-consuming. Having a "will not die" attitude can help entrepreneurs stay focused and see these projects through to completion, even when the going gets tough. Overall, having a **"will not die"** attitude can be an important mindset for entrepreneurs to have in order to succeed in the challenging world of entrepreneurship. It involves a determination to keep going and find creative solutions to overcome challenges, even when things seem insurmountable.

"
I'M CONVINCED THAT ABOUT HALF OF WHAT SEPARATES SUCCESSFUL ENTREPRENEURS FROM THE NON-SUCCESSFUL ONES IS PURE PERSEVERANCE.

STEVE JOBS

Persistence and perseverance:

Persistence and perseverance are important qualities for entrepreneurs to have because starting and running a business can be challenging and involves a lot of hard work and dedication. It is not uncommon for entrepreneurs to face setbacks and challenges along the way, and having the ability to persevere through these challenges is crucial for success.

Here are a few ways in which persistence and perseverance can be beneficial for entrepreneurs:

Overcoming setbacks and challenges: Entrepreneurs often face a variety of challenges and setbacks, such as financial difficulties, regulatory hurdles, and competitive pressures. Persistence and perseverance can help entrepreneurs keep going even when things get tough and find creative solutions to overcome these challenges.

Building resilience: Entrepreneurship can be a rollercoaster ride, and it's important to have the resilience to handle the ups and downs. Persistence and perseverance can help entrepreneurs develop this resilience and bounce back from failures or setbacks more quickly.

Seeing projects through to completion: Starting a business often involves taking on many different projects and tasks, some of which may be complex and time-consuming. Persistence and perseverance can help entrepreneurs stay focused and see these projects through to completion, even when the going gets tough.

Maintaining motivation: Being an entrepreneur can be demanding and it's important to stay motivated and focused on the long-term vision. Persistence and perseverance can help entrepreneurs stay motivated and keep working towards their goals, even when faced with setbacks and challenges.

Hence, persistence and perseverance are essential qualities for entrepreneurs to have in order to succeed in the challenging world of entrepreneurship.

SPEND TIME UPFRONT TO INVEST IN SYSTEMS AND PROCESSES TO MAKE LONG-TERM GROWTH SUSTAINABLE.

JEFF PLATT

Systems and processes:

There are several reasons why entrepreneurs should develop and implement effective systems and processes in their businesses:

Improved efficiency: Systems and processes help to streamline the way work is done, reducing the time and effort required to complete tasks. This can help to increase productivity and efficiency, allowing businesses to operate more smoothly and effectively.

Enhanced consistency: Systems and processes help to ensure that work is completed in a consistent and predictable manner, which can improve the quality and reliability of products and services.

Better communication: Systems and processes help to clearly define roles and responsibilities, which can improve communication and collaboration within a business.

Increased scalability: Effective systems and processes can help businesses to scale up more efficiently, as they provide a foundation for growth and expansion.

Enhanced organization: Systems and processes help to organize and structure the way work is done, making it easier for entrepreneurs and their teams to stay on track and meet deadlines.

Note: developing and implementing effective systems and processes can help entrepreneurs to run their businesses more smoothly and efficiently, enabling them to focus on growth and success.

YOU DON'T BUILD A BUSINESS, YOU BUILD PEOPLE, THEN PEOPLE BUILD THE BUSINESS.

ZIG ZIGLAR

Understanding human resources:

As an entrepreneur, understanding human resources (HR) is important for building and managing a successful team. HR involves managing and supporting the people who work for your business. It encompasses a wide range of activities, including recruiting and hiring employees, managing payroll and benefits, providing training and development opportunities, and enforcing company policies.

Effective HR management can help you attract and retain top talent, create a positive work environment, and ensure that your business is in compliance with labor laws and regulations. It can also help you resolve conflicts and manage employee performance.

Here are some key HR responsibilities that entrepreneurs should be familiar with:

Recruitment and hiring: This involves attracting and selecting the right candidates for open positions within your company.

Onboarding: This involves introducing new employees to your company and helping them get acclimated to their new roles.

Training and development: This involves providing employees with the knowledge and skills they need to perform their jobs effectively and efficiently.

Performance management: This involves setting performance goals for employees, evaluating their progress, and providing feedback and support to help them improve.

Employee relations: This involves building strong relationships with employees and addressing any issues or concerns they may have.

Payroll and benefits: This involves managing employee salaries, bonuses, and benefits such as health insurance and retirement plans.

Compliance: This involves staying up-to-date with labor laws and regulations and ensuring that your business is in compliance with all applicable laws.

By understanding and effectively managing these HR responsibilities, entrepreneurs can build a strong and successful team that is motivated and committed to the success of the business.

Understanding of financial concepts and principles:

As an entrepreneur, it is important to have a strong understanding of financial concepts and principles in order to effectively manage and grow your business. Some key financial understandings that entrepreneurs should consider include:

Profit and loss: Understanding how to read and analyze financial statements, such as a profit and loss (P&L) statement, is critical for understanding the financial health and performance of your business. A P&L statement shows your revenues, expenses, and net profit or loss for a specific period of time.

Cash flow: Cash flow refers to the movement of money into and out of your business. It is important to monitor and manage your cash flow carefully in order to ensure that you have enough money coming in to cover your expenses and meet your financial obligations.

Break-even analysis: This involves calculating the point at which your business is generating enough revenue to cover its costs, resulting in a profit. Understanding your break-even point can help you make informed decisions about pricing, production, and marketing.

Budgeting: A budget is a financial plan that outlines your expected income and expenses for a specific period of time. Creating and adhering to a budget can help you manage your finances more effectively and reach your financial goals.

Financial ratios: Financial ratios are useful tools for evaluating the financial performance and stability of your business. Some common financial ratios include the debt-to-equity ratio, the current ratio, and the return on investment (ROI).

Financing options: As an entrepreneur, you may need to explore different financing options in order to fund your business. This could include taking out loans, seeking investment from venture capital firms or angel investors, or crowdfunding.

By understanding these financial concepts and principles, entrepreneurs can make informed financial decisions that help their businesses succeed.

Understanding the fundamentals of operations:

As an entrepreneur, understanding the fundamentals of operations is essential for managing and growing a successful business. Operations refers to the processes and systems that a business uses to produce and deliver its products or services. Here are some key fundamentals of operations that entrepreneurs should be familiar with:

Process design: This involves identifying and optimizing the steps involved in producing and delivering your products or services. This includes determining the most efficient and cost-effective way to produce your products, as well as how to get them to your customers.

Capacity planning: This involves determining the maximum amount of products or services that your business can produce and deliver within a given time period. It is important to ensure that you have enough capacity to meet customer demand, but not so much that you are overproducing and incurring unnecessary costs.

Supply chain management: This involves managing the flow of raw materials, finished goods, and related information from suppliers to customers. Effective supply chain management can help you ensure that you have the materials you need to produce your products and that your products are delivered to customers in a timely and cost-effective manner.

Quality control: This involves implementing systems and procedures to ensure that your products or services meet the necessary standards of quality. This could include inspections, testing, and the implementation of quality management systems such as ISO standards.

Inventory management: This involves managing the stock of raw materials, finished goods, and other supplies that your business needs to produce and deliver its products or services. It is important to maintain an appropriate level of inventory to meet customer demand without incurring unnecessary holding costs.

By understanding these operations fundamentals, entrepreneurs can develop and implement effective systems and processes that help their businesses run smoothly and efficiently.

Understanding marketing and sales:

As an entrepreneur, understanding marketing and sales trends can be very important for several reasons:

Staying up-to-date on marketing and sales trends can help you identify new opportunities to reach and engage with potential customers.

Understanding trends can also help you anticipate changes in consumer behavior and adapt your marketing and sales strategies accordingly.

Knowing what is happening in the industry can also help you stay competitive and stay ahead of the curve in terms of the marketing and sales techniques and technologies you use.

Finally, understanding marketing and sales trends can help you make informed decisions about how to allocate your resources and budget, as well as how to position your products or services in the market.

Overall, staying informed about marketing and sales trends can help you be more effective in attracting and retaining customers, which is crucial for the success of any business.

Understanding social media and trends:

As an entrepreneur, it can be helpful to understand social media and trends in order to effectively market your business and connect with your target audience. Here are a few tips for understanding social media and trends as an entrepreneur:

Choose the right platforms: There are many different social media platforms available, each with its own unique audience and set of features. It's important to choose the platforms that are most relevant to your business and target audience.

Understand your audience: To effectively use social media, it's important to understand the demographics, interests, and behaviors of your target audience. This will help you create content that resonates with them and effectively reach them through social media.

Monitor trends: Social media trends can change quickly, so it's important to stay up-to-date on what's popular and relevant to your audience. You can use tools like Google Trends to track trends and see what topics are currently popular on social media.

Engage with your audience: Social media is a great way to connect with your customers and build a community around your business.

Make an effort to regularly interact with your followers and respond to comments and questions.

Use visual content: Visual content, such as photos and videos, tends to perform well on social media. Consider incorporating visuals into your social media strategy to increase engagement and reach.

By following these tips, you can effectively use social media to market your business and connect with your target audience.

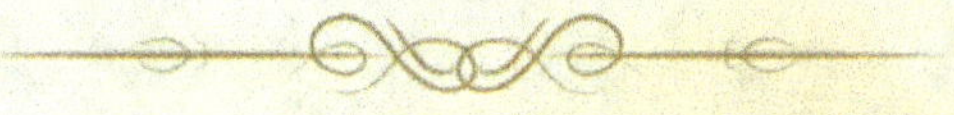

Understanding R.O.I

ROI, or **return on investment**, is a measure of the profitability of an investment. It is calculated by taking the gain from an investment (return) and dividing it by the cost of the investment (investment). A high ROI indicates that an investment is generating a good return for the amount invested, which is important for entrepreneurs to understand when making business decisions.

Entrepreneurs should have a good understanding of the expenses incurred by each department in their business and the ROI of those expenses in order to make informed decisions about budget allocation. This information can help them determine which departments and activities are most profitable and should be given priority in terms of funding. By tracking expenses and ROI by department, entrepreneurs can make more strategic decisions about where to invest their resources, which can help improve the overall profitability of the business. Additionally, it can help them to identify inefficiencies, non-performing departments and areas of the business that may require re-structuring.

Understanding Cost of customer acquisition (COCA)

Understanding the **cost of customer acquisition** (COCA) in a business is an important aspect of managing expenses and determining the overall profitability of a company. COCA is the cost incurred by a company to acquire a new customer, which includes expenses such as marketing, advertising, and sales efforts. By understanding COCA, a business can determine the effectiveness of their customer acquisition strategies and the return on investment for those strategies.

To calculate COCA, a business would take the total cost of customer acquisition efforts (such as marketing campaigns, sales salaries, advertising expenses) for a specific period of time and divide that by the number of new customers acquired during that period.

For example, if a company spent $50,000 on marketing and acquired 200 new customers, the COCA would be $250 per customer.

Lifetime value (LTV) of a customer

It is important to note that COCA should be compared with the lifetime value (LTV) of a customer, which is the total revenue that a customer generates for the company during their lifetime. A high COCA compared to LTV may indicate that a company's customer acquisition strategies are not cost-effective, and that the company may need to re-evaluate its approach to acquire new customers in a more efficient way.

Start off with a PLAN "A" but have a PLAN "B"

It's generally not a good idea to rely on a single plan or approach without any backup options. It's important for entrepreneurs to be flexible and adaptable, and to have contingency plans in place in case something goes wrong or unexpected challenges arise.

Having a **Plan B** can provide a fallback option if Plan A doesn't work out, and can help you to minimize risks and maximize your chances of success. It's important to be proactive in identifying potential risks and developing strategies to mitigate them. This can include having contingency plans in place for various scenarios, such as a supplier failing to deliver materials on time, a key employee leaving the company, or a natural disaster disrupting operations.

It's also important to stay agile and continuously reassess and adjust your plans as needed. The business landscape is constantly changing, and it's important to be able to Adapt and pivot as needed to stay competitive and achieve your goals.

Understanding S.W.O.T

SWOT analysis is a strategic planning tool used to evaluate the strengths, weaknesses, opportunities, and threats involved in a business or project. It is typically used to identify the internal and external factors that may affect the organization and to determine how to address them.

Strengths refer to the characteristics of the business or project that give it an advantage over others in the industry. These might include things like a strong brand, a highly skilled workforce, or a patent on a key technology.

Weaknesses are the opposite of strengths. They are characteristics of the business or project that may be viewed as disadvantageous when compared to competitors. Examples of weaknesses might include a lack of financial resources, a weak market position, or outdated technology.

Opportunities are external factors that may be favorable to the business or project. These might include new market opportunities, partnerships or collaborations, or changes in regulations or technology that create new avenues for growth.

Threats are external factors that may negatively impact the business or project. These might include competitors, changes in market conditions, or regulatory or technological changes that may pose challenges to the organization.

The goal of a SWOT analysis is to identify the key internal and external factors that are important to the success of the business or project, and to determine how to leverage the strengths and opportunities while minimizing the impact of the weaknesses and threats. This can help the organization to develop a plan to achieve its goals and to be more prepared to respond to challenges that may arise.

the effectiveness of a SWOT analysis depends on the specific goals, objectives, and context of the business or project. The key is to identify the strengths, weaknesses, opportunities, and threats that are most relevant to the organization and to use this information to inform strategic planning and decision-making.

In the early stages of a startup, it is especially important to be proactive in conducting a SWOT analysis and to be open to revising and updating the analysis as the business or project evolves. This can help the startup to identify and take advantage of new opportunities, to mitigate potential threats, and to build on its strengths as it grows and develops.

Understanding PIVOT

In business, **a pivot is a strategic move in which a company changes its business model, target market, or product offering** in order to adapt to new market conditions or customer needs. Pivoting can be a way for a company to stay competitive and find new sources of revenue or growth. It can also be a way for a company to recover from a difficult situation, such as declining sales or market disruption. Pivoting can be a risky move, as it involves making significant changes to the way a company operates, but it can also be a necessary step in order to survive and thrive in a rapidly changing business environment.

Here are a few examples of famous companies that have undergone a pivot:

Twitter: Twitter originally started as a podcasting platform called Odeo before pivoting to the social networking site we know today.

Groupon: Groupon was originally a platform for organizing political campaigns before pivoting to a daily deals site.

Slack: Slack was originally a game called Glitch before pivoting to a business communication platform.

Instagram: Instagram was originally a location-based social networking app called Burbn before pivoting to a photo-sharing app.

YouTube: YouTube was originally a dating site called Tune In Hook Up before pivoting to a video-sharing platform.

"

WITHOUT A PLAN, EVEN THE MOST BRILLIANT BUSINESS CAN GET LOST. YOU NEED TO HAVE GOALS, CREATE MILESTONES AND HAVE A STRATEGY IN PLACE TO SET YOURSELF UP FOR SUCCESS.

YOGI BERRA

KEY POINTS OF WRITING AN EFFECTIVE BUSINESS PLAN

Executive Summary

The Business

The Market
Market Analysis
Market Segmentation
Strengths
Weaknesses
Target Audience
Competition

Strategies
Marketing Strategies
Sales Strategies
Strategic Alliances

The Management Structure
Key Players
Organization Chart
Staffing Costs

The Financial Plan
Needs Summary
Revenue Model
Assumptions and Comments

APPENDICES

Implementation Schedule and Milestones

Further Development / phase 2

Exit Strategy

Why is it important to write a business plan?

Writing a business plan is an important step in the process of starting a business. A business plan is a document that outlines the goals of a business, the strategies that will be used to achieve those goals, and the resources that will be needed to implement those strategies. It also includes financial projections and a description of the target market.

There are several reasons why it is important to write a business plan before starting a business:

It helps to clarify your business idea and determine its feasibility. A business plan forces you to think through all aspects of your business and determine whether it is viable.

It helps to identify potential risks and develop strategies to mitigate them. By identifying potential risks and developing contingency plans, you can minimize the impact of those risks on your business.

It helps to attract investors and secure financing. A well-written business plan can be used to attract investors or secure financing from a bank or other financial institution.

It serves as a roadmap for your business. A business plan acts as a roadmap for the direction of your business and helps to keep you on track as you work to achieve your goals.

It helps to build credibility. A business plan demonstrates that you have thought through your business idea and are serious about making it a success.

In short, a business plan is an essential tool for any entrepreneur who wants to start a business. It helps to clarify your business idea, identify potential risks, attract investors, and serve as a roadmap for the direction of your business.

Understanding each of the business plan points:

A **market analysis** is an essential component of a business plan. It helps to identify the target market for a business, assess the size and growth potential of the market, and understand the competition.

Here are some key points to include in a market analysis for a business plan:

Description of the target market: Who are the potential customers for the business? What are their characteristics (age, income, location, etc.)?

Size of the target market: How large is the target market in terms of potential customers and revenue?

Market trends: What trends are currently affecting the market, and how might they impact the business?

Competition: Who are the major competitors in the market? What are their strengths and weaknesses?

Market segmentation: How can the target market be segmented into smaller groups with similar characteristics?

Marketing strategy: How will the business reach and persuade potential customers to buy its products or services?

Market growth: What is the current and projected growth rate for the market? How does this compare to the overall economy?

Barriers to entry: What challenges or obstacles will the business face in entering the market?

By thoroughly analyzing the market, a business can gain a deep understanding of the opportunities and challenges it will face, and develop a strategy to effectively reach and serve its target customers.

Strengths and weaknesses:

It is important to consider both your strengths and weaknesses when writing a business plan because it helps you to identify areas where you have an advantage over your competitors and areas where you may need to improve. By understanding your strengths, you can better position your business to take advantage of opportunities and achieve your goals. For example, if you have strong financial management skills, you might want to highlight this strength in your business plan as a way to demonstrate to potential investors or lenders that you have the ability to manage the financial aspects of your business effectively.

On the other hand, it is also important to be honest about your weaknesses and to identify areas where you may need to improve. By acknowledging your weaknesses, you can take steps to address them and improve your chances of success. For example, if you lack marketing skills, you might want to consider hiring someone with expertise in this area or seeking out resources to help you develop these skills.

Knowing your target audience and competitors is also critical when writing a business plan. Understanding your target audience will help you to tailor your products or services to meet their needs and preferences. It will also help you to identify potential market opportunities and to develop effective marketing strategies.

Similarly, understanding your competitors will help you to differentiate your business and to identify areas where you have a competitive advantage. It will also help you to anticipate their actions and to develop strategies to respond to them.

Overall, considering your strengths, weaknesses, target audience, and competitors is essential for developing a successful business plan and for positioning your business for success in the market.

Market segmentation:

Market segmentation is a process of dividing a market into smaller groups of consumers with similar needs or characteristics. As an entrepreneur, it's important to understand market segmentation because it can help you identify and target specific groups of consumers more effectively. This can be especially useful if your business caters to a wide range of consumers, as it allows you to create more targeted marketing campaigns and tailor your product or service offerings to the specific needs and preferences of each segment.

There are several different ways to segment a market, including:

Demographic segmentation: This involves dividing the market based on characteristics such as age, gender, income, education level, and geographic location.

Psychographic segmentation: This involves dividing the market based on consumers' attitudes, values, lifestyles, and personality traits.

Behavioral segmentation: This involves dividing the market based on consumers' behavior and their use of the product or service.

Benefit segmentation: This involves dividing the market based on the benefits that consumers are seeking from a product or service.

It's important to note that market segmentation is not a one-time process, but rather an ongoing process that entrepreneurs should constantly be revisiting and refining as their business grows and the market changes.

SOMETIMES WHEN YOU INNOVATE, YOU MAKE MISTAKES. IT IS BEST TO ADMIT THEM QUICKLY, AND GET ON WITH IMPROVING YOUR OTHER INNOVATIONS.

STEVE JOBS

Target audience:

Understanding your target audience is an essential part of starting and running a successful business. It allows you to tailor your marketing and sales efforts to the specific needs and characteristics of your intended customers, and to create products and services that are more likely to meet their needs and preferences.

To understand your target audience, you should begin by defining who your ideal customer is. Consider factors such as age, gender, location, income level, education level, interests, and values. You can use this information to create a detailed customer profile or "buyer persona" that represents your ideal customer.

Once you have defined your target audience, you should try to learn as much as possible about them. This might involve conducting market research, gathering data on your existing customers, or engaging with potential customers through surveys, focus groups, or other methods. You can also use social media, online forums, and other platforms to learn more about your target audience and get feedback on your products or services.

By understanding your target audience, you can create a more targeted and effective marketing and sales strategy, and design products and services that are more likely to meet the needs and preferences of your intended customers.

Be aware of competition

As an entrepreneur, it is important to **be aware of competition** in your market. This can help you make informed decisions about your business strategy and positioning.

There are a few key ways to stay informed about competition:

Research your market: Conduct market research to understand the competitive landscape in your industry. This can include identifying key competitors, understanding their products or services, and analyzing their pricing, marketing, and distribution strategies.

Monitor your competitors: Keep an eye on your competitors' activities, such as new product launches, changes to their business model, or shifts in their marketing strategy. You can use tools like Google Alerts to stay informed of any news or updates about your competitors.

Analyze your competitors' strengths and weaknesses: Understand what your competitors do well and what areas they may be lacking in. This can help you identify opportunities to differentiate your business and target specific areas for improvement.

Stay up to date with industry trends: Keep an eye on industry trends and stay current on new developments in your field. This can help you identify new opportunities and stay ahead of the competition.

By staying aware of competition and continuously adapting to changes in the market, you can position your business for success

Being aware of competition in order to be competitive:

As an entrepreneur, it is important to be aware of competition in order to be competitive in your market. Here are a few key strategies to stay competitive in the face of competition:

Offer a unique value proposition: Identify what sets your business apart from your competitors and make it clear to your target audience. This could be through unique products or services, a strong brand, or excellent customer service.

Monitor and adapt to market trends: Stay up to date on industry trends and be ready to adapt your business strategy accordingly. This could involve introducing new products or service revising your pricing strategy, or updating your marketing efforts.

Invest in marketing and promotion: Make sure your target audience is aware of your business and what you have to offer. This can involve targeted marketing efforts, such as social media advertising or content marketing, as well as more traditional forms of promotion, like print or radio advertising.

Foster strong relationships with customers: Building strong relationships with customers can help you retain their loyalty and keep them coming back. This can involve offering excellent customer service, following up with customers after a purchase, and responding promptly to any issues or concerns they may have.

By staying aware of competition and continuously adapting to changes in the market, you can position your business for success and stay competitive in the face of competition.

Understanding Marketing strategies, sales strategies, & strategic alliances:

Marketing strategies, sales strategies, and strategic alliances are important elements of a business plan because they help a business define how it will reach its target customers, generate revenue, and achieve its overall objectives.

Marketing strategies outline the plan for promoting and selling products or services to customers. This can include tactics such as advertising, public relations, social media marketing, and other forms of outreach. Marketing strategies help businesses identify who their target customers are, what their needs and preferences are, and how to communicate with them effectively.

Sales strategies outline the plan for converting leads into customers. This can include tactics such as pricing, promotion, and sales channels. Sales strategies help businesses identify how they will reach their target customers, what their value proposition is, and how they will close deals.

Strategic alliances are partnerships or collaborations with other businesses or organizations that can help a company achieve its goals. These alliances can be useful in a variety of ways, such as sharing resources, accessing new markets, and leveraging complementary skills and expertise.

Overall, marketing, sales, and strategic alliance strategies are important because they help businesses define how they will grow and succeed in the marketplace. They provide a roadmap for generating revenue, reaching new customers, and achieving long-term objectives.

Management structure and Key players

Planning the management structure, key players, organization chart, and staffing costs are important elements of a business plan because they help a business define how it will be organized and run on a day-to-day basis.

The management structure outlines the hierarchy of decision-making within the company, including the roles and responsibilities of different levels of management. This can help a business ensure that it has the right leadership in place to make strategic decisions, oversee operations, and manage employees effectively.

Key players refer to the individuals who will play a critical role in the success of the business. This may include the founders, key executives, and other important stakeholders. It's important to identify these key players and outline their roles and responsibilities in the business plan because they will be responsible for driving the company's growth and success.

An organization chart is a visual representation of the management structure and key players in a company. It shows the relationships between different levels of management and the responsibilities of each role. An organization chart can help a business understand how different parts of the company fit together and how decisions are made.

Knowing appropriate staffing costs is also important because it helps a business understand how much it will cost to hire and retain employees. This includes not only salary and benefits, but also other costs such as training, office space, and equipment. Understanding staffing costs is critical for budgeting and financial planning, and it can help a business ensure that it has the resources it needs to build a strong team.

Basics of what an investor looks at before investing

Typically, an investor looks at several key factors before deciding to invest in a company. These include the team behind the company, the market opportunity for the product or service, the company's business model and revenue potential, and the company's ability to execute on its plan. Additionally, investors will often look at the company's intellectual property and the strength of its competitive positioning in the marketplace. Due to the high risk nature, investor also often look at the size of the market opportunity and the potential for large returns on their investment.

So before you plan to rise funds make sure your business plan is put in place and you know what exactly you are rising the funds for.

Fundamentals of planning to raise funds to start your business

Debt financing is a type of funding in which a business borrows money from a lender, such as a bank or credit union. This can take the form of a traditional loan, which involves borrowing a specific amount of money upfront and paying it back with interest over a set period of time. A line of credit is another type of debt financing, which involves borrowing a specific amount of money, but allows the business to borrow and repay the funds as needed, rather than all at once.

Equity financing involves selling ownership stakes in the business in exchange for capital. This can be done through the sale of stocks, which allows the business to raise capital by issuing shares of ownership to investors. Private investments, such as those from angel investors or venture capital firms, are another form of equity financing. In this case, the business sells a portion of ownership in the company to the investor in exchange for capital. While equity financing allows businesses to access capital without taking on debt, it also means giving up a portion of ownership and control of the company.

Grants are another option for businesses seeking funding. These are typically provided by government agencies or non-profit organizations and are often given to businesses that align with their mission or values. Grants do not need to be repaid, but they may come with certain requirements or restrictions, such as the need to report on the use of the funds or the requirement to follow certain guidelines or regulations

Crowdfunding is a method of raising capital that involves soliciting small investments from a large number of people, usually through an online platform. This allows businesses to tap into a wider pool of potential investors and raise money more quickly than traditional methods, such as seeking investments from a small number of venture capital firms. However, crowdfunding can also be a competitive and unpredictable way to raise money, as businesses must be able to effectively market their ideas and attract a sufficient number of investors.

Ultimately, the best funding option for a business will depend on its specific needs and goals. Entrepreneurs should carefully consider the pros and cons of each type of funding before making a decision.

Common attributes that may make a business more attractive to potential lenders or investors when seeking financing:

- ➤ **A solid business plan:** A comprehensive and well-written business plan can demonstrate to lenders or investors that the business has a clear vision, defined goals, and a plan for achieving success.

- ➤ **Strong financials:** Potential lenders or investors will often want to see evidence of the business's financial stability and viability. This may include things like financial statements, cash flow projections, and profit and loss statements.

- ➤ **A track record of success:** A business that has already achieved some level of success may be more attractive to lenders or investors than a new start-up with no track record.

- ➤ **A competitive advantage:** A business that can demonstrate a unique value proposition or competitive advantage may be more appealing to lenders or investors.

- ➤ **A strong management team:** A business with a strong and capable management team can inspire confidence in potential lenders or investors.

- ➤ **A clearly defined market:** A business that has identified a specific target market and has a clear plan for reaching and serving that market may be more attractive to lenders or investors.

- ➤ **Collateral:** Some lenders may require collateral, such as property or assets, to secure a loan. A business that has strong collateral may be more attractive to lenders

It is important to note that these are just some of the common attributes that may make a business more attractive to potential lenders or investors. The specific requirements and criteria for financing will vary depending on the lender or investor and the specific needs of the business

Bootstrapping in business refers to the practice of starting and growing a business with very little or no outside funding. This means that the business owner or founders use their own personal resources, such as savings or credit, to finance the business. Bootstrapping is often seen as a way to maintain control and ownership of the business, as the owner is not beholden to any outside investors or lenders.

There are several benefits to bootstrapping a business, including:

Retaining ownership and control: By using their own personal resources to finance the business, the owner can retain complete ownership and control of the company.

Avoiding debt: Bootstrapping can help a business avoid taking on debt, which can be beneficial in the long run as the business will not have to worry about repaying loans with interest.

Forced efficiency: Bootstrapping can encourage a business to be more efficient and resourceful, as the owner must carefully manage their resources and make every dollar count.

Flexibility: Without the constraints of outside investors or lenders, a business that is bootstrapped may have more flexibility to pivot and change direction if needed.

However, there are also **challenges to bootstrapping** a business. It can be difficult to secure the necessary resources and capital to get the business off the ground, and the business may have to rely on personal resources, such as credit cards or loans, which can be risky. Additionally, the business may have limited access to the capital and expertise that can be provided by outside investors.

Ultimately, whether or not bootstrapping is the right choice for a business will depend on the specific needs and goals of the business and the availability of personal resources.

Seeking external financing, or obtaining funding from sources outside of the business, can have both advantages and disadvantages for a business.

Some advantages of seeking external financing include:

Access to larger amounts of capital: External financing can provide a business with access to larger amounts of capital than the business may be able to secure through personal resources or profits.

Expertise and guidance: External investors, such as venture capital firms or angel investors, may bring valuable expertise and guidance to the business.

Increased credibility: Obtaining funding from outside sources can increase the credibility of the business, which may make it more attractive to customers and other potential partners.

Potential for faster growth: With access to additional capital, a business may be able to scale and grow more quickly.

Seeking external financing can also have some disadvantages, including:

Loss of ownership and control: In exchange for funding, a business may have to give up a portion of ownership and control to the investor.

Debt: Some forms of external financing, such as loans, require the business to take on debt, which must be repaid with interest.

Loss of flexibility: Investors may have specific requirements or expectations for the business, which can limit its flexibility and decision-making power.

Risk of failure: If the business is not able to meet the expectations of its investors, it may risk losing its funding and potentially facing financial hardship.

Ultimately, whether or not seeking external financing is the right choice for a business will depend on the specific needs and goals of the business and the availability of personal resources. It may be necessary for a business to seek external financing if it requires a significant amount of capital or expertise that the owner does not have.

Importance of a financial plan:

A financial plan is an important component of a business plan that outlines the company's expected financial performance over a specific period of time, typically several years. Some key points to include in a financial plan are:

Projected income statements: These show the company's expected revenues, costs, and profits over time.

Projected balance sheets: These show the company's expected financial position, including assets, liabilities, and equity, at a specific point in time.

Projected cash flow statements: These show the company's expected cash inflows and outflows over time, including the sources and uses of cash.

Funding needs: This section should outline the company's anticipated funding needs, including how much capital it will need to raise and when it will need it.

Financial assumptions: This section should outline the assumptions that underlie the financial projections, such as sales growth rates, cost of goods sold, and expenses.

Break-even analysis: This analysis shows the point at which the company's revenues will cover its costs and it will start to make a profit.

Overall, a financial plan is important because it helps a business understand its financial performance and position over time, and it provides a roadmap for achieving financial goals. It also helps investors and lenders understand the company's financial projections and assess its financial viability

Understanding the needs and intent of the business

The needs summary is an important element of a business plan because it clearly and concisely outlines the key needs that the business aims to address. This can include the needs of the target market, the needs of the business itself, and any other relevant needs.

For example, the needs summary may include information about the problems or challenges that the target market is facing, and how the business's products or services will solve those problems. It may also include information about the company's own needs, such as funding or partnerships, and how those needs will be met.

The needs summary is important because it helps the business articulate its value proposition, or the unique benefits that it offers to customers. It also helps the business clearly define its target market and understand the needs of that market.

In addition, the needs summary is often the first section of a business plan that investors or lenders will read, so it's important to make a strong and compelling case for the business's value proposition. A well-written needs summary can help convince potential investors or lenders that the business is worth supporting.

Understanding of a revenue model:

A clear understanding of a revenue model is important while writing your business plan because it helps you to determine how your business will generate revenue and make a profit. It is a key component of your financial plan and can help you to understand the potential financial performance of your business. A revenue model also helps you to determine the pricing of your products or services, the cost of delivering them, and the resources you will need to sustain your business.

Having a well-defined revenue model can also be helpful when seeking funding from investors or lenders, as it demonstrates to them how your business will generate income and become financially viable. A clear and realistic revenue model can also help you to identify potential risks and challenges that you may encounter as you try to grow your business.

A clear understanding of your revenue model is essential for the success of your business, as it helps you to make informed decisions about how to generate income and achieve your financial goals.

Importance of assumptions:

There are several assumptions that you can base your business plan on, including:

Market demand: You can make assumptions about the size and growth of the market for your products or services, as well as the demand for those products or services.

Customer demographics: You can make assumptions about the characteristics of your target customers, such as their age, income, location, and interests.

Competition: You can make assumptions about the competitive landscape in your industry, including the number and types of competitors you will face and their relative strengths and weaknesses.

Pricing: You can make assumptions about the pricing of your products or services, including the factors that will influence your pricing decisions and any price elasticity that you may encounter.

Costs: You can make assumptions about the costs of producing and delivering your products or services, including the cost of materials, labor, and any other expenses you will incur.

Sales and marketing: You can make assumptions about the strategies and tactics you will use to reach and sell to your target customers, as well as the resources you will need to do so effectively.

Financial performance: You can make assumptions about your financial performance, including your revenue, expenses, and profit margins, as well as any financing you will need to support your business.

It is important to note that these assumptions should be based on sound research and analysis, and should be revisited and updated as needed as your business evolves.

Planning your implementation:

An implementation schedule is a detailed timeline that outlines the specific steps and activities that are required to achieve the goals and objectives of your business plan. It is important to include an implementation schedule in your business plan for several reasons:

It helps to break down complex tasks into smaller, more manageable steps: An implementation schedule can help you to break down complex tasks into smaller, more manageable steps that are easier to execute and track.

It allows you to allocate resources effectively: By creating an implementation schedule, you can identify the resources that are required to complete each step of your plan, and allocate those resources accordingly.

It helps you to track your progress: An implementation schedule allows you to track your progress and measure your success against specific milestones and deadlines. This can help you to identify any problems or delays in your plan and adjust your approach accordingly.

It helps to keep your team focused and motivated: An implementation schedule can help to keep your team focused and motivated by providing them with a clear set of goals and deadlines to work towards.

Overall, an implementation schedule is an essential tool for helping you to execute your business plan effectively and achieve your goals. It allows you to plan and coordinate the various activities that are required to launch and grow your business, and to track your progress and measure your success along the way.

Planning Exit Strategy

An exit strategy is an important component of a business plan because it outlines how the business will eventually be sold or transitioned to new ownership. This can include a plan for an initial public offering (IPO), a merger or acquisition, or a sale to a private equity firm. Having an exit strategy in place can help attract investors, as they will have a clear understanding of how they will eventually see a return on their investment. Additionally, an exit strategy can also help the business owner plan for their own eventual exit from the company, whether it be retirement or moving on to another venture.

All the successful people irrespective of the fields they represent in this world have emphasized on this particular fact

If you want success, "You have to be comfortable not being comfortable.

Understanding few of the different business models:

There are many different business models that companies use in the present world. Some common business models include:

1. **Manufacturer:** A business that produces goods to be sold to customers.

2. **Wholesaler:** A business that buys goods in large quantities from manufacturers and sells them to retailers.

3. **Retailer:** A business that buys goods from wholesalers or manufacturers and sells them to consumers.

4. **Service provider:** A business that provides a service to customers, rather than a physical product. Examples include consulting firms, law firms, and healthcare providers.

5. **Franchise:** A business model in which a company (the franchisor) licenses its brand, products, and operating systems to other businesses (the franchisees) in exchange for a franchise fee and a percentage of the franchisee's sales.

6. **Subscription:** A business model in which customers pay a regular fee in exchange for access to a product or service.

7. **E-commerce:** A business model in which a company sells products or services online.

8. **Peer-to-peer (P2P):** A business model in which individuals or companies offer products or services directly to customers, rather than through a traditional business.

9. **Sharing economy:** A business model in which individuals or companies use technology to share access to goods or services, rather than owning them outright. Examples include ride-sharing and home-sharing platforms.

10. **Social enterprise:** A business that is driven by a social or environmental mission, in addition to generating profits.

Starting a manufacturing business can be a complex and challenging process. Here are some key points to keep in mind:

Develop a solid business plan: A business plan will help you define your target market, identify your competition, and outline your financial projections.

Research your market: Understand the demand for your product, the competition, and the regulatory environment in your industry.

Choose a location: Consider factors such as access to raw materials, transportation, and the availability of skilled labor when selecting a location for your manufacturing business.

Obtain financing: Determine the type of financing that is best for your business and start working on securing it. This may include loans, grants, or equity investments.

Assemble a team: Hire experienced and skilled employees to help you design, produce, and market your products.

Choose the right production process: Consider factors such as the complexity of your product, the scale of production, and the level of automation when selecting a production process.

Establish relationships with suppliers: Build relationships with reliable suppliers to ensure a steady supply of raw materials and other resources.

Invest in quality control: Establish processes to ensure that your products meet the highest standards of quality and safety.

Plan for growth: As your business grows, you may need to expand your production capacity, hire additional employees, or enter new markets. Be prepared to adapt to changes in the market and industry.

There are several key factors to consider when **starting a wholesale business:**

Identify your target market: It's important to have a clear understanding of who your target customers are and what products they are looking for. This will help you focus your efforts and ensure that you are offering the right products at the right prices.

Develop a strong business plan: A well-written business plan will help you set goals, allocate resources, and forecast future profits. It will also be useful when seeking funding from investors or lenders.

Secure funding: Depending on the size and scope of your wholesale business, you may need to secure funding to get started. This could include loans, grants, or investment from friends and family.

Find reliable suppliers: Building relationships with reliable suppliers is critical to the success of a wholesale business. You'll want to find suppliers who can offer high-quality products at competitive prices and who are willing to work with you to meet your specific needs.

Set competitive prices: In order to be successful, you'll need to set prices that are competitive with other wholesale businesses in your market. This will require research and analysis to determine the right balance between cost and price.

Promote your business: It's important to get the word out about your wholesale business, so be sure to utilize a variety of marketing and advertising tactics to reach potential customers. This could include social media, email marketing, and traditional advertising methods like print or radio ads.

Build a strong team: As your wholesale business grows, you'll need a strong team to help manage operations and support your customers. Look for talented, motivated individuals who share your vision for the business.

There are several types of **retail businesses**, including:

Brick-and-mortar stores: These are physical stores that customers can visit to browse and purchase products.

Online stores: These are virtual stores that customers can visit via the internet to browse and purchase products.

Pop-up shops: These are temporary retail spaces that are set up for a short period of time, often to promote a specific product or event.

Mobile retail businesses: These are retail businesses that operate out of a vehicle or portable space, such as a food truck or a mobile boutique.

Catalog or direct mail businesses: These are retail businesses that sell products through a catalog or direct mail order.

Franchises: These are retail businesses that are owned and operated by individuals who have purchased the right to use the business's name, products, and operating systems.

There are several key factors to consider when starting a retail business, including:

Identify your target market: It's important to have a clear understanding of who your target customers are and what products they are looking for. This will help you focus your efforts and ensure that you are offering the right products at the right prices.

Develop a strong business plan: A well-written business plan will help you set goals, allocate resources, and forecast future profits. It will also be useful when seeking funding from investors or lenders.

Secure funding: Depending on the size and scope of your retail business, you may need to secure funding to get started. This could include loans, grants, or investment from friends and family.

Find reliable suppliers: Building relationships with reliable suppliers is critical to the success of a retail business. You'll want to find suppliers who can offer high-quality products at competitive prices and who are willing to work with you to meet your specific needs.

Set competitive prices: In order to be successful, you'll need to set prices that are competitive with other retail businesses in your market. This will require research and analysis to determine the right balance between cost and price.

Promote your business: It's important to get the word out about your retail business, so be sure to utilize a variety of marketing and advertising tactics to reach potential customers. This could include social media, email marketing, and traditional advertising methods like print or radio ads.

Build a strong team: As your retail business grows, you'll need a strong team to help manage operations and support your customers. Look for talented, motivated individuals who share your vision for the business.

There are many different types of **service businesses**, including consulting firms, law firms, healthcare providers, repair and maintenance businesses, and more. Some factors to consider before starting a services business include:

Demand for your services: Research the market to understand the demand for your services and the competition.

Skills and expertise: Consider your skills and expertise, as well as those of any potential team members, to determine the types of services you can offer.

Equipment and resources: Determine the equipment and resources you will need to provide your services, and make sure you have the necessary funding to obtain them.

Pricing: Establish a pricing strategy that reflects the value of your services and allows you to be competitive in the market.

Marketing and promotion: Develop a marketing and promotion plan to reach potential clients and showcase the value of your services.

Legal considerations: Research the legal requirements for starting and operating a service business in your location, including any licenses or permits you may need.

Insurance: Consider the types of insurance you will need to protect your business, such as liability insurance to cover claims from clients.

Client relationships: Establish systems for managing client relationships, including processes for communication, billing, and dispute resolution.

A franchise business model is a type of business in which the owner (the franchisor) allows a third party (the franchisee) to use its trademarks, intellectual property, and business model in exchange for a fee. The franchisee agrees to operate their business according to the franchisor's established systems and processes, and to adhere to the franchisor's standards for products and services.

There are several key points to consider when starting a franchise business:

Research: It's important to thoroughly research the franchise opportunity and the franchise industry before making a commitment. This includes reviewing the franchise disclosure document, which provides information about the franchise system, the franchise agreement, and the franchisor's business experience.

Financing: Franchises typically require a significant upfront investment, which may include the franchise fee, training costs, and start-up expenses. You'll need to determine how you will finance your franchise, which may involve seeking loans or investment from family, friends, or financial institutions.

Location: Choosing the right location for your franchise is crucial. You'll need to consider factors such as demographics, competition, and accessibility.

Training and support: Most franchisors provide training and ongoing support to their franchisees, including marketing and operational support. It's important to understand what support will be provided and how it will be delivered.

Legal considerations: You'll need to carefully review and understand the terms of the franchise agreement, which outlines the rights and responsibilities of both the franchisor and the franchisee. You may also want to consult with an attorney or franchise consultant to ensure that you fully understand the agreement and the risks involved.

Starting a franchise business requires careful planning, research, and due diligence. It's important to understand the obligations and risks involved, and to ensure that you have the necessary resources and support to succeed. And most important factor of all is to be responsible to investors who trust your brand and come forward to associate with you in the hope of a brighter future.

A subscription business model is a type of business model in which customers pay a recurring fee to access a product or service on a regular basis. The product or service can be a physical product, a digital product, or a combination of both. Customers typically sign up for a subscription and agree to pay a fixed fee on a regular basis, such as monthly or annually.

There are a few key factors to consider when starting a subscription business:

Product or service: First, you need to decide what product or service you will offer as part of your subscription. This could be a physical product, such as a monthly box of organic produce, or a digital product, such as a subscription to a software service.

Pricing: Determine how much you will charge for your subscription and how often you will charge (e.g., monthly, quarterly, annually). Consider the cost of producing and delivering your product or service, as well as the value it provides to your customers.

Customer acquisition: You will need to develop a marketing and sales strategy to attract and retain customers for your subscription business. This may include creating a website, building a social media presence, or working with affiliates or partners to promote your product or service.

Customer retention: Retaining customers is critical for a successful subscription business. You will need to consistently deliver high-quality products or services and provide excellent customer service to keep your customers coming back.

Billing and payment: You will need to set up a system for billing and collecting payments from your customers. This may include integrating with a payment processor or setting up recurring billing through your website or e-commerce platform.

Legal and compliance: Make sure you are complying with all relevant laws and regulations, including those related to consumer protection and privacy. You may need to consult with a lawyer or other legal professional to ensure you are in compliance.

Starting an e-commerce business involves a lot of planning and decision making. Here are some key factors to consider when starting an e-commerce business:

Product or service: First and foremost, you need to decide on the product or service you want to sell. This will be the foundation of your business, so it's important to choose something that you are passionate about and that meets a need in the market.

Target market: Who is your target market? Understanding your target market will help you identify the best marketing strategies and channels to reach them.

Competition: It's important to understand your competition, including their products, pricing, and marketing strategies. This will help you position your business in the market and identify areas where you can differentiate yourself.

Marketing and sales: How will you reach and sell to your target market? Consider which marketing channels will be most effective for your business, such as social media, email marketing, and search engine optimization.

E-commerce platform: You'll need to choose an e-commerce platform to host your online store. There are many options available, including Shopify, WooCommerce, and Magento.

Payment processing: You'll need to choose a payment processor to handle transactions on your website. Options include PayPal, Stripe, and Square.

Shipping and fulfillment: How will you handle shipping and fulfillment for your products? Will you handle it yourself or use a fulfillment service?

Legal and compliance: Make sure you understand and adhere to all relevant laws and regulations, including those related to taxes, data privacy, and consumer protection.

Finances: Carefully plan and manage your finances, including creating a budget and forecasting your revenue and expenses.

Starting an e-commerce business requires a lot of effort and planning, but it can also be a rewarding and profitable venture.

Key factors to consider when starting a **peer-to-peer (P2P) business**:

Market demand: It is important to identify a market need or demand for the product or service you plan to offer. This will help ensure that there is a sufficient customer base for your business.

Competition: It is also important to assess the level of competition in the market. This will help you determine the feasibility of your business idea and identify potential areas of differentiation.

Business model: You will need to develop a clear and viable business model that outlines how your P2P business will operate and generate revenue. This should include details on how you will match buyers and sellers, as well as any fees or commissions you will charge.

Legal and regulatory considerations: P2P businesses are subject to a variety of legal and regulatory requirements. It is important to understand and comply with these requirements to avoid any legal issues or penalties.

Technology: P2P businesses often rely on technology to facilitate transactions and connect buyers and sellers. It is important to choose the right technology and platforms to support your business.

Customer service: P2P businesses rely on positive customer experiences to drive growth and success. It is important to have a strong customer service strategy in place to ensure that you are able to effectively address customer needs and concerns.

The sharing economy is a business model in which individuals can borrow or rent assets owned by someone else. These assets can be physical products, such as cars or bicycles, or intangible services, such as accommodations or professional services. The sharing economy allows people to access resources that they may not have access to otherwise, or that they may not want to own themselves.

There are several factors to consider when starting a sharing economy business:

Market demand: It's important to assess the demand for the product or service you are offering. Is there a need for it in the market? Are there already other businesses offering similar products or services?

Business model: There are several different business models within the sharing economy, including peer-to-peer platforms, rental platforms, and subscription-based models. Consider which model is best suited to your business.

Legal and regulatory considerations: Sharing economy businesses are subject to various legal and regulatory considerations, including taxes, insurance, and licensing requirements. It's important to understand these requirements and ensure that your business is in compliance.

Safety and liability: Sharing economy businesses often involve the exchange of physical goods or services, which can come with risks. It's important to consider how to manage these risks and ensure the safety of your customers and assets.

Customer service: In the sharing economy, customer service is key. Customers expect a seamless, convenient experience when using your product or service. It's important to have a solid customer service plan in place to ensure that you are able to meet these expectations.

Marketing and promotion: Marketing and promotion are important for any business, but in the sharing economy, it's especially important to differentiate your product or service from competitors. Consider how you will reach your target audience and promote your business.

A social enterprise is a business that has a social or environmental mission at its core. The profits from the business are used to achieve this mission, rather than being distributed to shareholders or owners.

There are several key factors to consider when starting a social enterprise:

Mission: Clearly define your social or environmental mission and how it will be achieved through the business.

Target market: Identify your target market and understand their needs and how your product or service will meet those needs.

Business model: Determine the best business model for your social enterprise, such as a nonprofit, a for-profit with a social mission, or a hybrid model.

Funding: Identify potential sources of funding, including grants, loans, and investments, and develop a solid financial plan.

Legal structure: Choose the appropriate legal structure for your social enterprise, such as a corporation, partnership, or sole proprietorship.

Team: Assemble a strong team with the skills and expertise needed to successfully launch and run your social enterprise.

Marketing and outreach: Develop a marketing and outreach plan to effectively communicate your mission and value proposition to potential customers and stakeholders.

Impact measurement: Develop a system for measuring and reporting on the social or environmental impact of your business. This can help you track progress and demonstrate the value of your work to funders and other stakeholders.

Financial services business model

There are several different business models that financial service companies can use. Some common ones include:

Retail banking: Retail banks offer traditional banking services such as checking and savings accounts, credit cards, and loans to individuals and small businesses. These banks typically generate revenue through fees, interest on loans, and service charges.

Investment banking: Investment banks provide a variety of services to their clients, including underwriting and issuing securities, providing advisory services, and trading in financial markets. They typically generate revenue through fees and commissions.

Asset management: Asset management companies offer investment management services to individuals and institutions. They typically generate revenue through management fees and performance-based fees.

Insurance: Insurance companies provide risk protection to individuals and businesses by offering policies that cover a wide range of risks, including health, property, and liability. They generate revenue through premiums paid by policyholders.

Peer-to-peer lending: Peer-to-peer (P2P) lending platforms match borrowers with investors who are willing to lend money directly to them. P2P lenders generate revenue through origination fees and interest on loans.

Crowdfunding: Crowdfunding platforms allow individuals and businesses to raise funds from a large number of people, typically through the internet. These platforms typically generate revenue through fees charged to campaign organizers and backers.

Payment processing: Payment processing companies facilitate electronic transactions between merchants and customers. They generate revenue through fees for processing transactions.

There are many other financial service business models as well, and some companies may use a combination of these models to generate revenue.

Business is a vast and ever-changing field, and new business models are constantly emerging as the world changes. Some of the key trends driving the development of new business models include the increasing use of technology, changes in consumer behavior, and shifts in global economic conditions.

One of the most significant impacts of technology on business has been the rise of e-commerce and digital platforms. Online marketplaces, such as Amazon and Alibaba, have disrupted traditional retail businesses by making it easier for consumers to find and purchase goods from a wide range of sellers. Digital platforms, such as Uber and Airbnb, have also disrupted traditional industries by connecting consumers with providers of goods and services in new ways.

Another key trend driving the development of new business models is changes in consumer behavior. As consumers become more environmentally and socially conscious, they are increasingly looking for products and services that align with their values. This has led to the emergence of new business models, such as social enterprise, that focus on achieving social or environmental impact in addition to generating profits.

Finally, shifts in global economic conditions have also played a role in the development of new business models. For example, the rise of the sharing economy, in which people share access to goods and services rather than owning them outright, has been driven in part by the economic downturn of the late 2000s and the subsequent rise of the gig economy.

Hence, it's important for businesses to stay aware of these trends and to be open to new and innovative business models as they emerge. It's also important to remember that there's no one-size-fits-all approach to business, and that the best business model for a particular company will depend on a variety of factors, including its industry, target market, and competitive landscape.

Repeating this page to emphasis the importance of understanding tvhis point

A good business plan **doesn't guarantee success** of your business **but it certainly increases** the chances of success

"MAKE SOMETHING PEOPLE WANT" INCLUDES MAKING A COMPANY THAT PEOPLE WANT TO WORK FOR.

SAHIL LAVINGIA

Conclusion

As an entrepreneur, it is important to remember that progress, not perfection, is key. Perfection is an ongoing process that is constantly evolving and is never fully achieved. Instead of focusing on being perfect, focus on making progress and taking small steps towards your goals. And never have self-doubt, believe in yourself and your abilities. It is important to push through these doubts and keep moving forward in order to achieve success.

A business plan is a critical tool for any entrepreneur. It outlines the goals and strategies needed to achieve success. This book provides a clear roadmap to help business owners make informed decisions and stay on track to reach their objectives. It provides a comprehensive guide to help you create a successful business plan, as well as the knowledge to enable you to reach your goals and fulfill your dreams of being a successful entrepreneur.

Wishing you the best life can give

Thanks for reading

SresQUEST

The quest for knowledge, understanding, and progress is a fundamental trait of humanity. It is what drives us to explore, to innovate, and to create. It is the quest for a better life, for ourselves and for future generations. It is the quest for new discoveries and breakthroughs in science, technology, medicine, and art. It is the quest for personal growth and self-improvement. Without the quest, humanity would have never achieved the incredible advances and accomplishments that we have today. The quest is the engine that keeps us moving forward, and it is vital to our continued growth and evolution as a species.

It is true that history is written by the winners, but it is also true that failures give us valuable experiences that can help us become better and more successful in the future. It is important not to lose confidence and to keep going, even after a defeat. This is the key to success - to never give up and to keep striving for your goals.

sharing my experiences and knowledge with aspiring entrepreneurs through this book on the "Entrepreneur's Guide to Business Plan." A guide on how to create a comprehensive and effective business plan can be a valuable resource for those looking to start their own business. My experience and insights will bring valuable perspective through this book, and can help aspiring entrepreneurs avoid common mistakes and navigate the challenges of starting a business. Hence helping to empower and inspire the next generation of entrepreneurs to pursue their own business ventures with confidence and success.

SresQUEST